Analyzing Collapse

The AUC History of Ancient Egypt

Edited by Aidan Dodson and Salima Ikram

Volume Two

Analyzing Collapse

The Rise and Fall of the Old Kingdom

Miroslav Bárta

The American University in Cairo Press
Cairo New York

First published in 2019 by
The American University in Cairo Press
113 Sharia Kasr el Aini, Cairo, Egypt
200 Park Ave., Suite 1700, New York, NY 10166

Dar el Kutub No. 26095/16
ISBN 978 977 416 838 3

Dar el Kutub Cataloging-in-Publication Data

Bárta, Miroslav
    Analyzing Collapse: The Rise and Fall of the Old Kingdom /
Miroslav Bárta.—Cairo: The American University in Cairo Press, 2019.
    p.   cm.
    ISBN: 978 977 416 838 3
    1- Egypt — History — Old Kingdom, ca. 2686–ca. 2181 B.C.
    932.013

1 2 3 4 5   23 22 21 20 19

Designed by Jon W. Stoy
Printed in The United States of America

Contents

Preface

I first came to Egypt in 1991 as an undergraduate student of Egyptology and prehistoric archaeology at Charles University in Prague. The fall of that year was my first excavation in Abusir, a rural site among the pyramid fields, but one of the principal sites of the Old Kingdom period. It proved to be crucial for my future career in many ways.

There I experienced the thrill of observing how monuments, built millennia ago and now fallen into oblivion, were reappearing from the sands of the desert. Such discoveries challenged my imagination and my ability to piece together small fragments of evidence to build a picture of the past. Step by step, as the days passed, the ancient Egyptian world was becoming more and more tangible. Destinies of individual officials were gaining more concrete contours. Their fates started to fill in the outlines of the world they lived in and which they helped to shape. Individual lives of long-forgotten Egyptian officials of both high and lower standing, together with the general characteristics of the Old Kingdom society, were merging together; the micro- and macro-worlds started to form a unified and tightly interwoven whole. It took me quite a long time to reach this level of perception, and I have no doubt that to arrive at a complete state of knowledge and understanding of such a complex society is utterly impossible. This book is an attempt to offer my present perspective on one of several important periods of ancient Egyptian history—one of the first complex civilizations in the history of this planet. This book is a kind of interim testimony to the development of that society.

But ambitious as this sounds, there is yet another aspect of this pursuit that I wish to share: individual archaeological discoveries represent an indispensable micro-world from which a general picture of historical processes several centuries long may be reconstructed. Ancient Egyptian evidence may be viewed from the *longue durée* perspective. This is an approach formulated by the French School of Annals; it refers to the study of history through mapping and analyzing evidence for specific historical processes over long periods of time, combined with individual historical events and with a strong multidisciplinary component.[1] Only this specific approach of addressing historical issues by means of multidisciplinary research may have significant relevance for comparative studies with other known civilizations. Certainly, each civilization attested on this planet was or is specific and there are no algorithms that could compare them on a unified basis. Equally, there is no way our past can predict our future. Still, past civilizations were shaped and maintained by people like us, people with minds like ours, who were faced with many phenomena we know from our own contemporary world. It is above all the inner dynamics of any given society which offers many points for comparison: rising complexity; growing and proliferating bureaucracy; the role of the state and its eventual erosion; the role of nepotistic structures and interest groups in controlling energy resources and competing with the declining state structures for power and dominance; the importance of the elites and what happens when they fail to perform their duties.[2] These are just a few phenomena which can be encountered in any given civilization, in any age or location.[3] In the same manner, the ways in which any civilization adapts to a changing environment constitute yet another universal phenomenon which has been intensively studied.[4] All these aspects combined indicate why it is that archaeology sometimes appears to be political. This results from a simple observation, namely that archaeology addresses most of the issues and processes (some of the most important of which are mentioned above) which are present in our own modern world. In fact, multidisciplinary study of the past has become an increasingly strategic discipline, and the analysis of history of *longue durée* combined with a detailed analysis of

Fig. 0.1. Visual metaphor of modern study of history. Tiled windows in the cathedral in Rheims by Marc Chagall. In order to create such impressive windows, each of the colored tiles must be carefully produced; each on its own would be meaningless. To understand any civilization one must do the same—combine single events and *longue durée* analysis. (M. Bárta)

individual historical events, with their environmental background and dynamism, is beginning to claim more space in research and is receiving increasing attention from science as such.[5] The same is true of the comparative study of civilizations.[6] Last but not least, since Joseph Tainter's pioneering and still influential study of collapses in different societies and civilizations, it is considered productive to study the mechanisms of crises in which archaeology and history play a dominant role.[7]

Therefore, my focus throughout the book will be the following seven rules, which appear to form the essence of every civilization of which we have knowledge, and which can be distilled from comparative study of complex civilizations and *longue durée* history.

Law One

Every civilization is defined in space and time. It has geographical borders and temporal limits. Archaeology and history are the disciplines that analyze the emergence, rise, apogee, crisis, eventual collapse (understood as a sudden and deep loss of complexity), and the transformations leading to their new evolution. The making and unraveling of any civilization is a procedure that emphasizes the idea of time and process in combination with human agency.

Law Two

Every civilization develops by means of a punctuated equilibria mechanism, according to which major changes happen in a non-linear, leap-like manner when the multiplier effect is present.[8] Once periods of stasis separating individual leap periods become shorter or disappear completely, one expects a major system's transformation, most often a sudden and steep loss of complexity (metaphorically called 'collapse').

Law Three

Every civilization uses a language that is universally understood by its members (its lingua franca, typically English in our Western world) and a commonly accepted system of values and symbols. Every civilization has major centers characterized by a concentration of population, monumental architecture, a writing system (in most cases), sophisticated systems of communication, systems for storing and sharing knowledge, a hierarchically shaped society, arts, and a division of labor. It also has the ability to redistribute main sources of energy—in other words, it has elites who are able to establish and maintain the so-called social contract and allow the majority of the population to share in the profits generated by the system, which is controlled by a minority with decisive power.

Law Four

If the prevalent tendency within the civilization favors consumption of energy over producing it and investing it in a further increase of complexity, there is a declining energy return on investment (EROI). It means that a coefficient gained from the amount of energy delivered by a specific energy resource (such as water, sun, atom, gas, or coal) divided by the amount of energy necessary to be used in order to obtain that energy resource is becoming less and less significant, and therefore less economically profitable. As a consequence, the original level of complexity cannot be sustained or expanded. Eventually, in leaps rather than gradually, the system will lose its existing complexity and implode. This is what is traditionally and inaccurately called a 'collapse.'

Law Five

Individual components of a given civilization proliferate and perish through inner mechanisms inherent in the society (changing bureaucracy, quality of institutions, role of the elites and technologies, ideology and religion, mandatory expenses, social system, and so on), and through the ability of the civilization to adapt to external factors such as environmental change. These are the internal and external determinants that shape the dynamics of any given civilization. They are in permanent interaction, in cycles of varying length.

Law Six

The so-called Heraclitus Principle has a major impact on all civilizations: the factors that promote the rise of civilizations are, more often than not, identical with those that usher in their collapse. Thus if we want to understand the precise nature and causes of the collapse, we must study not only the final stage of the system but its very incipient stage, where the roots of the future crisis usually lie.

Fig. 0.2. Visual metaphor of a collapse. Impressive sarcophagus chest left behind in a corridor in the sacred animal cemetery of Serapeum, Saqqara, Egypt, Ptolemaic period. The sarcophagus, which was to contain the body of the sacred Apis bull, never reached its final destination. The works, the faith, the legitimacy of the painstaking work ceased literally overnight; all workers and officials participating in this process walked away on a single day. This is what is typically called a collapse—sudden loss of complexity, lack of economic means, lost legitimacy, and erosion of commonly shared values compromising the social contract. (M. Bárta)

Law Seven

A civilization disappears at the moment when its system of values, symbols, and communication tools disappears, and when the elites lose their ability to maintain the social contract. Yet the collapse does not necessary imply extinction. In most cases, a civilization that has consumed its potential gives way to a new one, usually carried on by the same or a slightly modified genetic substrate of the original population. Collapse in this context is a positive phenomenon, as it removes dysfunctional parts of the system.

All the features in the above seven laws play a role throughout the following chapters, and I leave it to readers to judge their effect and relevance. The study of civilizations in the manner indicated above may in fact turn into strategic directions of research in the years to come. These laws are capable of describing long historical processes from the incipient stage of a civilization through its rise, apogee, decline, collapse, transformation, and reemergence.[9] Ancient Egypt underwent this cycle at least three times. The study of the rise and fall of the era of the Old Kingdom pyramid builders in multidisciplinary perspective is just a limited part of the large mosaic of human history, but it may prove to be valuable as a description and evaluation of a complex society from its rise to its demise over several centuries, and provide an analysis of its internal and external dynamics.

I would like to thank all my friends and colleagues who read first versions of this text and contributed immensely to its completion—Salima Ikram, Aidan Dodson, and Guy Middleton. I am grateful to Miroslav Verner, Jiří Melzer, and Vivienne G. Callender for many valuable comments, criticisms, and insightful remarks during the process of the work on the manuscript. I also want to thank all my colleagues in the Czech Institute of Egyptology, without whom I would not have been able to complete the necessary research for this book. The American University in Cairo Press provided an excellent environment for the finalization of the manuscript. I owe a lot to just a few persons, and they know who they are.

The work on this book was accomplished within the framework of the Charles University Progress project Q11: "Complexity and Resilience: Ancient Egyptian Civilization in Multidisciplinary and Multicultural Perspective."

The present book and research builds on the Czech publication which appeared in 2016 under the title *Příběh Civilizace. Vzestup a pád doby stavitelů pyramid* (Academia).

Chronological Table

(based largely on Hornung, Krauss, and Warburton 2006: 490–98)

Early Dynastic Period	c. 2900–2592[±25] BC
First Dynasty Narmer, Hor-Aha, Djer, Djet, Den, Anedjib, Semerkhet, Qaa	c. 2900–2730[±25] BC
Second Dynasty Hetepsekhemwy, Raneb, Ninetjer, Peribsen, Sekhemib, Sened, Khasekhemwy	c. 2730–2590[±25] BC
Old Kingdom	c. 2592–2120[±25] BC
Third Dynasty Netjerykhet Djoser, Sekhemkhet, Khaba, Nebka, Huni	c. 2592–2544[±25] BC
Fourth Dynasty Sneferu, Khufu, Djedefre, Khafre, Menkaure, Shepseskaf	c. 2543–2436[±25] BC
Fifth Dynasty Userkaf, Sahure, Neferirkare Kakai, Raneferef, Shepseskare Isi, Niuserre Ini, Menkauhor, Djedkare Isesi, Unas	c. 2435–2306[+25] BC
Sixth Dynasty Teti, Userkare, Pepy I Meryre, Nemtyemsaf Merenre I, Pepy II Neferkare, Nemtyemsaf Merenre II, Neitiqerti (Nitokris)	c. 2305–2118[+25] BC
Eighth Dynasty attested kings such as Neferkaure, Neferkauhor, Neferirkare	c. 2150–2118[±25] BC
First Intermediate Period	c. 2118–1980[±25] BC
Ninth and Tenth Dynasties Herakleopolitan rulers, some with the name Akhtoy	c. 2118–1980[±25] BC
Middle Kingdom	c. 1980[±16]–1760 BC
Eleventh Dynasty	c. 2080–1940[±16] BC
Twelfth Dynasty	1939[+16]–1760 BC
Second Intermediate Period	1759–c. 1539 BC
New Kingdom	c. 1539–1077 BC
Third Intermediate Period	c. 1076–723 BC
Late Period	c. 722–332 BC
Greek Rulers	332–305 BC
Ptolemaic Period	305–30 BC
Roman Period	30 BC—AD 395

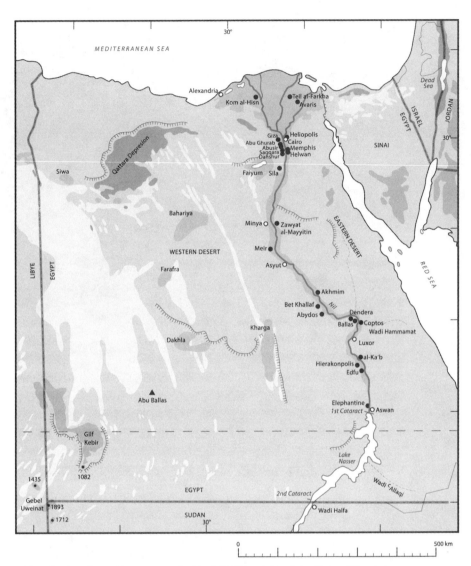

Map. Ancient Egypt. Source: compiled by J. Malátková, Czech Institute of Egyptology

1 Opening Up the Path: How Complex Societies Rise and Fail

Civilizations are dynamic; they rise and fall; they divide and merge. And, as any student of history knows, civilizations disappear and are buried in the sands of time.[1]

THIS STUDY IS DEVOTED to the anatomy of the emergence, rise, and decline of the first ancient Egyptian state—the Old Kingdom, which lasted from the twenty-seventh through the twenty-second centuries BC. During this period, the foundations of ancient Egyptian civilization, which survived for millennia, were laid, elaborated, and refined. Egypt was a gift of the desert and of a global environmental change (the desiccation of the Sahara), but also, to a much greater degree, as the ancient Greek historian Herodotus wrote, a gift of the Nile, whose annual flood cycle provided the Egyptians with an enormous amount of energy that supported the emergence, sustenance, and growth of their civilization. Agriculture in the Nile Valley was an extraordinarily high-return activity. The accumulation of wealth that it generated led to the rise of a complex hierarchical society with a powerful elite class, which enabled the construction of costly state projects imbued with symbolic power.

This society's internal dynamics, combined with climatic cycles and the characteristics of the Nile's flow, defined many features of ancient Egyptian civilization, from the way in which it operated to the principles

1

of its continuity and longevity. Ancient Egypt shows that a civilization can last as long as its founding ideas are kept alive. The Old Kingdom has been chosen as the core theme of this book because it was during this period that the main pillars were formed which would support ancient Egyptian civilization for the next two millennia.

The reader will certainly remember the sometimes dull history lessons at school, when past cultures and civilizations were presented as long lists of buildings, kings, dynasties, and officially relevant dates. Symbols were often used to represent thousands of years of human development, such as, for Egypt, Khufu's pyramid at Giza or Tutankhamun's tomb in the Valley of the Kings, or for Mesopotamia, the Code of Hammurabi or the royal cemetery of Ur.

Naturally, ancient Egyptian civilization offers much more than that. Human history is a long and continuous journey reflecting the endless curiosity of the human mind, a path that is exemplified in the history of Egypt. This chapter will attempt to examine in some detail the way states (as major building blocks of a mature civilization), including ancient Egypt of the Old Kingdom, emerge, develop, and eventually fail. It will address many ways these processes are made manifest, explore the internal and external factors that influence long-term developmental trends, and examine whether, and to what degree, such processes may be continuous or marked ('punctuated') by sharp and sudden breaks. It will be demonstrated that the era of the pyramid builders is fascinating not just for its birth and rise but also for how and why it failed.

What Is Civilization?

At the end of the nineteenth century it was a relatively common belief that the difference between civilization and earlier stages of human social organization, represented by bands or tribes, was the ability to write.[2]

As we now know from early Mesopotamia and the Bronze Age Aegean, script originated as a means to record accounting details such as the place of origin and quantity of various commodities.[3] Only later did writing develop into a form that could be used to record speech and abstract ideological concepts. Moreover, certain early civilizations (in the Mexican highlands, Peru, West Africa) developed a complex hierarchical society and civilization despite not using script.[4] Thus, writing alone is not the key to understanding the nature and origins of civilization, although it plays a major role.

The Australian archaeologist Vere Gordon Childe (1892–1957) sought to understand civilizations by identifying their characteristics.[5] He produced a list of ten major traits:

1. Large urban centers;
2. Craftsmen, merchants, clerks, and priests living on the surplus provided by farmers;
3. Primary producers submitting their surplus to a deity or king;
4. Monumental architecture;
5. A ruling class exempted from manual labor;
6. A system for recording information;
7. Exact sciences for practical purposes;
8. Monumental art;
9. Regular import of different materials—luxury goods as well as raw materials for production; and
10. Specialized craftsmen controlled politically and economically by secular or religious officials.

Of course there are exceptions to every rule, and it pays to be wary of didactic generalization. In his monumental *A Study of History*, the historian Arnold Toynbee (1889–1975) emphasizes that every civilization is singular and that development is always specific in many ways and different every time.[6]

A modern analysis of civilizations would thus query whether Childe's individual traits are really universal. Nonetheless, more than sixty years later his reasoning still seems correct in principle.[7] Indeed, many modern studies dealing with early civilizations have focused on the very traits he identified, while adding to them at the same time. There are, for instance, broader discussions of the roles played by conflicts and armies, the institution of royalty, the family and kinship ties, and law in the development of civilizations, together with ideology and the role of an elite headed by the monarch.

Bruce Trigger, in his monumental opus *Understanding Early Civilizations*, argues convincingly against relying on lists to understand as

Fig. 1.1. Pyramids in Giza. These incredible monuments not only embody the ability and potential of the Egyptian Old Kingdom; they also manifest one of the pillars of Egyptian ideology and religion. (M. Bárta)

complex a system as a civilization. Yet he falls into the same habit when he attempts to characterize civilizations on the basis of social, economic, and political institutions.[8] And although recent research is dominated by arguments that favor multidisciplinary approaches to defining the 'essence' of a civilization, it seems that one cannot avoid at least some reliance on tentative lists of essential traits, however relative and prone to modifications such lists may be. The argument favoring multidisciplinary approaches for defining an 'essence' of a civilization, however, seems to dominate the recent research on the subject which is, nevertheless, not free of bias and one-sided statements.[9]

The development of a civilization and its attendant socioeconomic complexity requires an interaction among most of these essential traits, which influence one another in a multiplier effect, as defined by Colin Renfrew.[10] Without this, even if we have cities sprawling over hundreds of hectares in front of our eyes, it is very difficult to speak about civilization as such if there is no sign of social stratification, such as diversified architecture, socially specific artifacts, stratified settlements, religious centers, significant long-distance trade, or specialized production. The recently much-discussed towns of the Cucuteni–Trypillian culture in Ukraine, which thrived between 5200 and 3500 BC, may serve as a typical example of an entity with very low complexity.[11]

It is appropriate now to look at traits commonly displayed by the ancient Egyptian civilization. The following attributes characterize ancient riverine civilizations in general, and have been applied to ancient Egypt in particular.[12]

- It was territorial and maintained its borders;
- At the time of unification, it was strong enough to be able to invest profits into the specialization of labor and into expansion, which led to further rapid social differentiation and specialization;
- It had an advanced system of written communication that enabled the gathering, storing, and sharing of information throughout the state (the Egyptian script began to develop well before the unification of the country);[13]
- At its origins it had a hierarchical social structure consisting of four principal social strata (typical model: king, courtiers, local power representatives, majority population);
- It was characterized by partial urbanism (existence of towns and large residential agglomerations) and was able to provide for and organize the settlement of new territories under its jurisdiction and control;
- It had an advanced material culture displaying a considerable degree of standardization and homogeneity;
- It operated on commonly recognized norms of behavior;
- It engaged in long-distance trade to import otherwise inaccessible raw materials, which enabled the elites to demonstrate their privileged status;
- It had an elaborate state ideology and religious system that defended the status quo established during the fourth-millennium Naqada II, if not earlier, which depended on ideology, theology, and divine intent, all formulated to emphasize first the chieftain's, and later the king's, exclusive relationship with the gods;[14]

- It had a developed court culture, which identified power through symbols and religion, as exemplified by monumental architecture and art;
- It implemented projects, especially in monumental architecture, which served on the one hand to justify the existence and privileged status of the monarch and ruling class and, on the other, as a way for the ruling class to share and redistribute a part of its wealth among the lower classes, thus committing most of the population to participate in, develop, defend, and preserve the established system;
- It was able to exercise power and oversight within its entire territory, as shown by many texts, the iconography of the period, and the administrative titles of administrators;
- It deployed judicial institutions and a legal system to settle disputes, which helped to reduce the chaos that unavoidably accompanies the growth of state complexity;
- It was able to wage war beyond the borders of its own territory.[15]

For the archaeologist Colin Renfrew, a civilization is a recurring group of artifacts of a particular kind, a unique way that a specific group of people have adapted within defined temporal and geographic boundaries. According to Samuel Huntington, a civilization is characterized by its specific identity.[16] But while the features that characterize different civilizations may vary, each includes most of the features listed above. This may prove helpful in understanding the similarities. Civilization is thus necessarily a polythetic entity.[17]

Compared to ancient Egypt, the (city or regional) states of the Near East developed quite differently during the fourth and third millennia BC.[18] Drawing on archaeological research about communities east of the fertile floodplain of the Tigris and Euphrates (the Susian Plain), American archaeologists Henry T. Wright and Gregory H. Johnson produced a theoretical concept of the state, distinguishing between a complex society organized at state level and less complex structural units, such as chiefdoms.[19] Their reasoning started from the basic observation that Egypt, like the region along the lower course of the Tigris and Euphrates, preserved archaeological material providing evidence of significant settlement hierarchy. There were usually several—at least three—tiers of settlements (for instance center, minor center, and village). They concluded from a separate analysis of seal impressions and other administrative evidence that these could only constitute a state, as commonly understood, when the leader or chief (later king) had mediators (later members of the court and 'ministerial' officials) by his side to transfer decisions to the next (third or possibly even further) tier(s).[20]

Linked to this development was another essential characteristic of the state: the ability to collect and keep information with the help of a system of writing. This information served as the basis for decision-making controlled by the elites, which enabled decisions to be implemented in a unified way. At its inception, script gave unrivaled advantage: it recorded data and provided any reader with the same data in an unaltered, objective form, exactly as it had been recorded. This model suggests that societies in the Nile Valley, southern Mesopotamia, and southwestern Iran had reached the state phase of development as early as the end of the fourth millennium BC.[21]

The Genesis of a State and the Social Contract

The genesis of the state has fascinated scholars both ancient and modern. For example, Aristotle (384–322 BC) considered the existence of the Greek-type *polis* to be natural and automatic, assuming that a state naturally results from the self-organizing principle of an increasingly complex society.[22]

As our understanding of the human past has grown, however, so has our awareness that the situation today is more complex in some regards, especially as the birth of a state is the outcome of many phenomena and their various combinations.[23]

An approach not too distant from Aristotle's can be found in early modern philosophy. Thomas Hobbes (1588–1679) was, in his 1651 book *Leviathan*, one of the first modern writers to deal with the idea of the genesis of the state. Hobbes believed that a state is formed due to man's need to protect himself against imminent war. That is why he creates the state ('commonwealth') and enters a 'social contract' under which he surrenders his individual freedoms and power for the benefit of the higher entity. This process is not, however, fully automatic or voluntary; coercion plays a significant role.[24]

In principle, Hobbes distinguishes three forms of state: monarchy, if power is in the hands of one individual; aristocracy, if power is held by an assembly composed of a restricted group of people; and democracy, if decision-making processes are approved by all citizens.

Similar ideas were developed by John Locke (1632–1704) in his *Second Treatise of Government* (1690). According to Locke, the state is formed to ensure peace and security and human rights, including individual property rights: the state is an arbiter duty-bound to ensure that the property of its individual members is protected.

These schools of thought were taken up freely in the eighteenth century by the French philosopher Jean-Jacques Rousseau (1712–78) in *Du contrat social, ou Principes du droit politique*, first published in Amsterdam in 1762. Rousseau held the view that a state emerges as the result of the conclusion of a social contract when "each of us puts his person and all his power in common under the supreme direction of the general will; and in a body we receive each member as an indivisible part of the whole."[25] Although this implies a voluntary act, there is a coercive element to this theory, too, as Rousseau asserts that "whoever refuses to obey the general will shall be compelled to do so by the whole body. This means nothing less than that he will be forced to be free."[26]

In a similar vein, at the beginning of the twentieth century, the German sociologist Max Weber (1864–1920) defined the state as a human community that claims a monopoly on the legitimate use of physical force within a given territory.[27]

Unfortunately, all these views and theories have one thing in common: they reflect an abstract idea of the formation of a state rather than addressing the process through which a state emerges in real life. This may be due, at least in part, to the fact that in the seventeenth and eighteenth centuries not much was known about the history of civilizations. Since then, exhilarating advances in archaeology and cultural anthropology, especially in the twentieth century, have produced vital physical evidence about the development of past cultures. This has initiated a new wave of research into the origin of states and shed new light on the origins of complex states.

As our understanding of the human past has grown, however, so too has our awareness that the birth of a state is the outcome of many

Fig. 1.2. Catal Hüyük, Turkey (7500–5700 BC). One of the earliest cities in the world, with a population of up to 10,000. (reconstruction by P. Vavrečka)

phenomena in various combinations.[28] Current theories of the origin of the state can be roughly divided into two groups (albeit with fuzzy, overlapping boundaries): the first posits that a state is formed by voluntary unification of lower units, in a quasi-Aristotelian way; the second, that states are primarily coerced into being.

Childe theorized that the origins of the state were natural or noncoercive: that the introduction of agriculture and settled communities led to overproduction, which allowed segments of the population to specialize, as they were no longer needed for agriculture. This gave rise to a common need for such settled communities to come together and create larger and larger coalitions. Contemporary archaeological evidence shows that in the Near East this consolidation began as early as the fourth millennium BC in the form of the above-mentioned city-states, which were true centers of learning and crafts, as well as being the foci of the elite of that era.[29] On a general level, one might object that this is a grossly generalizing theory that does not take into account either the geography or the specific circumstances under which states originated, not to mention the fact that in many parts of the world, settled farming populations are known to have existed that never developed any

Fig. 1.3. Taxation of the whole territory of the Egyptian state was one of the principal prerequisites to build and maintain a highly complex society. Tomb of Mereruka, Saqqara, early Sixth Dynasty. (M. Bárta)

discernible system of government.[30] However, the evidence from Egypt and the Near East is rather convincing in this respect.

Karl Wittfogel (1896–1988), in his 1957 study, *Oriental Despotism: A Comparative Study of Total Power*, offered a different perspective based on the development of early civilizations in Mexico, China, Egypt, and Mesopotamia. Wittfogel argued that the basic impulse for the rise of all these civilizations was the need to organize labor in a large territory to implement the grand construction projects required to support agriculture in large river basins.

Wittfogel's theory was applied to Egypt several decades later by Karl Butzer (1934–2016), in his 1976 study *Early Hydraulic Civilization in Egypt: A Study in Cultural Ecology*, and by the German Egyptologist Wolfgang Schenkel, in his *Bewässerungsrevolution im Alten Ägypten* (1978).

It is evident today that while the origins of the Egyptian state really may have been linked to the need to deal with the annual flooding of the Nile, other cases (such as Mesopotamia) are not so clear-cut. And even as far as ancient Egypt is concerned, there is good reason to ask whether it was necessary to build irrigation projects of *such* size, for instance canals capable of distributing water over a wider territory than that affected directly by the Nile flood.

A more recent theory, proposed by Yale professor James C. Scott, is that early states could be established due to the new possibility of effective taxation that was enabled by developed agriculture, as grain taxation, collection, and redistribution were the most suitable means along which economies of the early agrarian states could be organized.[31]

War and Civilizations

In the present book there will be frequent references to the birth of the unified Egyptian state around the beginning of the third millennium BC. This has often been ascribed to wars waged by Upper Egyptian elites against their northern neighbors in line with the theories of the Enlightenment philosophers discussed above.[32] Like these earlier thinkers, the British sociologist Herbert Spencer (1820–1903), whose intellectual sources included the evolutionists Charles Darwin (1809–82) and Thomas Huxley (1825–95), also regarded the threat of war as the prime factor motivating the formation of states.[33]

In recent times, war or conflict has been a common focus of contemporary American economists and political scientists such as Douglass C. North, John Joseph Wallis, and Barry R. Weingast.[34] In many ways their work follows on from the ideas of the Enlightenment philosophers. Although their primary interests are the development of modern states and the modern phenomenon of war, they also deal with the effects of war and conflict on the development of populations since the agricultural revolution. They link their basic argument—which is not so different from Childe's—to the beginnings of agriculture: farming permitted the establishment of settled communities; unlike human groupings in earlier periods, these farming communities experienced rapid population growth, which naturally increased the potential for conflict over land, property, and influence.[35]

Roy A. Rappaport (1926–97), drawing on his research in Papua New Guinea, argued that even linear population growth can result in the exponential growth of the potential for conflict; he called it the "irritation coefficient."[36] While a nomadic group may have up to twenty-five members, a clan may have some two hundred and a tribe up to a thousand: social systems exceeding a thousand members are generally held to constitute chiefdoms. Comparative studies have looked at such groups in the real world, and they too regard war, or the growing threat of conflict, as being both directly dependent on population growth and the primary motivating factor in the formation of a state capable of exercising an exclusive monopoly on violence in its territory.[37]

It can thus be proposed that war, or the threat thereof, and the need to organize labor for large construction (and—yes!—irrigation) projects, which a small community would be unable to implement on its own, have been part of major driving forces behind the emergence of states. These factors will not have been exclusive causes, but their formative impact is beyond doubt.

Environmental and Social Circumscription Theories

The American anthropologist Robert Carneiro studied the diversity of the forms into which states develop, and in 1970 proposed an elaborate theory of the origin of the state. He noted that states have originated in diverse regions lying at different distances from the Equator, different heights above sea level, with different qualities of soil, temperatures, total rainfall, and many other variables. But he also observed that among all these variables, the states that developed in Mexico, Peru, Egypt, and the Middle East had one thing in common: the amount of land available for farming was constrained by sea, desert, or mountains. Carneiro refers to this feature as "environmental circumscription."

Carneiro developed his theory with a comparative analysis of two populations: agricultural communities in the Amazon lowlands and in the coastal lowlands of Peru. In the Amazon lowlands, the amount of agricultural land is almost limitless. Individual farming communities are dispersed over a large area; the distance between them is usually some fifteen to twenty-five kilometers. There were wars here, of course, but these were waged to demonstrate individual heroism, acquire women, or take personal revenge.[38] They were not primarily wars over land or property. Whenever a village was defeated, its inhabitants simply fled to another part of the forest to establish another settlement. Since there was a seemingly endless supply of agricultural land, there was no reason to forge military coalitions or organized, hierarchical units to defend or attack.

In contrast, agricultural land was the alpha and the omega of development for villages that had sprung up in the eighty or so valleys on the northern coast of Peru, which were constrained by the ocean, mountains, and desert. The settlement of these valleys expanded with the rising number of people living in the villages. Once a village population reached some three hundred people, some were dispatched to build a new village. The size of the individual villages thus remained fairly constant.[39] Once the valleys were settled, the pressure on land use increased.

Fig. 1.4. Monte Albán. One of the driving forces of the early states was wars. Monte Albán rulers managed to unify the whole territory of Oaxaca and thus increased their available resources. Zapotec civilization, Oaxaca valley, Mexico. (M. Bárta)

This led to existing land being cultivated more intensely or to new arable land being acquired by building terraces on steep slopes, although the latter required much more energy and resulted in a declining EROI (Energy Return On Investment, or the amount of energy that must be expended compared to the amount of usable energy that it creates).[40] Eventually these technical options were exhausted and economic stress led to aggression against neighbors. Such wars had serious consequences for the defeated communities, but they were the unavoidable result of the scarcity of available land combined with the practical impossibility of escape because of the desert, mountain, or sea barrier. This was the mechanism by which a strictly hierarchical society emerged, grew over time to encompass larger territories controlled by individual chiefs, and eventually developed into kingdoms—as happened, for instance, with the Inca Empire and its predecessors, like the Moche culture.[41] It was a process that led naturally to deep social stratification, the rise of a small and powerful elite, larger groups of professional clerks and craftsmen with some privileges, and finally, large groups of farmers and war captives with no privileges at all.

The theory that states emerge as a result of external environmental stress is paralleled by a theory of "social circumscription," a concept introduced by Napoleon Chagnon (b. 1938) based on populations in Amazonia, and particularly on the Yanomamo tribe.[42] A tribe of some ten thousand members, the Yanomamo live in the rainforest where there is an abundance of arable land. Nevertheless, as Chagnon notes, the individual villages of this tribe are not spread out evenly over the area: they are mainly concentrated in a clearly defined center, and settlements on the periphery are sparse. As a result, the villages in the center are larger in both size and population than those on the edges, closer to one another, and their leaders are stronger and wield more authority. Social tension in the center is much greater and, besides environmental stress, there is also deeper social stratification, with communities growing stronger internally because of continuous social pressure on space, authority, power, and carrying capacity.

Some Factors to Add

Alongside war and expansion and the construction of large-scale projects and monuments, the basic framework for the genesis of the early state included an ideology leading to the formation of an elite headed by a king or ruler of some sort, the need for trade—especially long-distance trade for the purpose of acquiring (among other things) prestigious artifacts and raw materials—and technological innovation.

Another key characteristic of the early state is a central government with the ability to maintain law and order, if necessary by force. This includes the ability largely to prevent internal conflicts and the division of the population into a governing minority and governed majority.

Last but not least, the state's basic function is to create a surplus, which is needed to keep the state running, to support the state ideology, and to redistribute some economic potential and wealth for the benefit of most of the population, and thus maintain a kind of simple social contract—at least, this was the case of early states, such as Egypt or the city-states of

Fig. 1.5. Army of Nubian soldiers. Famous models from the tomb of Mesehti, Asyut, First Intermediate Period. (M. Bárta)

the Near East. Recent cross-cultural comparative study by Richard E. Blanton and Lane F. Fargher goes further and indicates that state formation (and evolution) results from strategic behavior by rational and self-interested actors from both the political elite and the majority that is outside the state's official administrative structure which are—in the case of archaic states—mainly peasants. The result is that building collective polities can provide mutual benefits to all bodies involved.[43]

It must be stressed that when we talk about central government in relation to early states, we are not necessarily referring to the same degree of centralization and verticality as in the modern state. The most realistic model of ancient Egypt in the third millennium BC appears to consist of a relatively powerful center or capital (Memphis) capable of exercising local rule over the country's most significant local settlements, which overlapped with the most economically productive and strategically important regions.[44] There can be no doubt, however, that this center was able to concentrate and redistribute the large economic flows without which it would be difficult to imagine the construction of pyramid complexes and other projects, or the sustenance of a large priestly class (see chapters 6 and 7). Centralization as it is understood today—implying detailed control of the institutions and processes all over the state's territory—probably did not exist in Old Kingdom Egypt. It is more likely that organically evolving agglomerations emerged, where the power elite and the central institutions were concentrated. True, there was a major center in Memphis, but it coexisted with smaller centers across the country which were semi-independent. Everyday aspects of governance, including services in temples of local gods, and often carried out by traditional local families, blended in these towns with elements of presentation of royal power and ideology often personified by an official dispatched on the order of the king.[45] All this, of course, took place within environmental and geographical constraints.[46]

There is a danger in comparing civilizations and cultures thousands of kilometers and centuries apart. A separate temporal and spatial analysis of the social development of any given polity must be carried out and the processes that characterize it identified, described, and understood. Only then can an attempt be made to generalize the results.[47]

Huntington and Annual Rings

External factors other than war and geography may also have played a role in state formation. We will focus especially on one 'superfactor'—the changes of climate over time.

The quest to understand the climate and its relevance for the human population is not new. A *Hymn to the Nile* (also known as the *Hymn to Hapi*) dating to the New Kingdom (sixteenth to eleventh centuries BC) is clear proof that the Egyptians, too, were very much aware of how important this mighty natural source of water, energy, and transport was for them:

Adoration of Hapi:
Hail to you, Hapi,
Sprung from earth,

Come to nourish Egypt! . . .
Who floods the fields that Re has made,
To nourish all who thirst;
Lets drink the waterless desert,
His dew descending from the sky . . . .
When he floods, earth rejoices,
Every belly jubilates,
Every jawbone takes on laughter,
Every tooth is bared.
Food provider, bounty maker,
Who creates all that is good!
Lord of awe, sweetly fragrant,
Gracious when he comes.
Who makes herbage for the herds,
Gives sacrifice for every god . . . .
He fills the stores,
Makes bulge the barns,
Gives bounty to the poor.[48]

Mesopotamian literature also contains unique descriptions of climatic oscillations, which were thought to indicate divine displeasure with the human race. There is no lack of lively descriptions of consecutive years of crop failure and there can be no doubt that these descriptions are based in reality.[49]

Ibn Khaldun (1332–1406), a medieval author, in *The Muqaddimah: An Introduction to History*, addresses climate change and its effect on human populations in the harsh desert environment and the rich mountainous regions of the Maghreb (modern Morocco). According to Ibn Khaldun, the different geographical and climatic zones had a fundamental impact on the history of individual ethnic groups.[50] This was a precursor to the views of the French philosopher Charles Louis de Montesquieu (1689–1755), who believed the natural environment (among other things) shaped the nature and character of a specific society and determined whether it would be aggressive, peaceful, settled, nomadic, or agricultural. On that basis he concluded that a single political order could not apply to all societies.[51]

Fig. 1.6. Nile River. All early complex civilizations came into being in close proximity to major rivers. (M. Bárta)

One of the first modern works to deal with the supposedly causal relationship between climate change and civilization's development was the work of the American geographer Ellsworth Huntington (1876–1947), professor of geography at Yale. He observed that past waves of desiccation resulted in large migrations and also ultimately led to the collapse of the Roman Empire.[52] He was one of the first to measure and analyze, in 1911 and 1912, the annual rings of the Californian *Sequoiadendron giganteum* and draw a curve of climate fluctuations (dry and humid phases) between 1300 BC and AD 1900 on the basis of long-term rates of wood increment. He then drew a similar curve for western Asia, and by comparing the two, concluded that climate trends were global.[53]

There is a connection (probably unintended) between his work and that of Bedřich Hrozný (1879–1952), the renowned Czech archaeologist and linguist who deciphered Hittite, and in 1940 published a work titled *O nejstarším stěhování národů a o problému civilisace proto-indické* (On the migration of nations and issues of the Proto-Indian civilization) where he points to the desiccation of vast steppe regions in Asia as the main cause triggering the migration of nations.

Another scholar to argue that climate and history were linked was the American meteorologist Hurd C. Willett (1903–92). In studying the Holocene climate, he concluded that it was possible to identify approximately 1,850-year-long cycles characterized by a tendency toward warming or cooling.[54] Willet was among the first—at least of those known to the author—to deal with the concept of regular climatic cycles during the Holocene. He was soon followed by Rhys Carpenter (1889–1980), professor of classical archaeology at Bryn Mawr College, whose 1966 work *Discontinuity in Greek Civilization* is one of the first published historical studies focusing on the relationship between man and changing climatic conditions.

Bond and Climate Change

There has been further work since then on Holocene climate change, especially by Gerard Bond and his team,[55] who have found evidence that significant climate change occurred over a short period of time in a whole series of "events." Bond dated these to 9100, 8300, 7400, 6100, 3900, 2200, and 800 BC and AD 550, with a periodical incidence rate of approximately 1,470 years.[56] Thus, climatic oscillations during the Holocene occurred at approximately 1,500-year intervals. Each oscillation consisted of a gradual cooling and then a sharp drop in temperatures, followed by a cold period at the end of which temperatures rose steeply.[57]

In the ancient Egyptian context, a notable period is the one that dates roughly from 3000 BC to 2000 BC, the period of the second-largest Holocene change and tentatively equivalent to the Old Kingdom. This was a period of slow cooling that followed the climatic optimum in the early Holocene between 6200 BC and 3000 BC. Around 2500 BC there was an evident change in the trend—from the warmer and drier Sub-Boreal to a cooler and more humid Sub-Atlantic climate.[58]

Details of the second event are unknown, except that it was slower and culminated around 2200 BC.[59] This may have been the product of four different and mutually independent factors. The first to be mentioned is usually the radical cooling of the North Atlantic region. The second possible factor was the start of a 1,500-year-long oscillation period, and

Fig. 1.7. Climate change and fluctuations of the Holocene era. Climate has always had a significant impact on the character of civilizations and cultures. A protracted spell of droughts made the Anasazi culture disappear within several years at the end of the thirteenth century. Cliff palace, Mesa Verde, Colorado. (M. Bárta)

the third was a major El Niño–Southern Oscillation (ENSO) effect. The last could be the reaction of the atmosphere and vegetation to smaller orbital oscillations of the Earth.[60]

Collapses and the History of Ancient Egypt

This book is concerned mainly with the search for and description, evaluation, and interpretation of the processes leading to the birth, rise, and finally fall of the Egyptian Old Kingdom. Having evaluated some general aspects of the birth of civilizations, we must now discuss—in a necessarily limited manner—some general features associated with the famous and often misunderstood phenomenon of 'collapse.'[61]

Collapse has frequently been represented by an archetypal myth, most often in the form of a deluge or other large-scale natural event that annihilates a culture. Evidence of this myth and its different variants appears independently in many civilizations and cultures around the world, including ancient Egypt and the Middle East, early China, and Australia.[62] The common denominator of all these myths is a gigantic disaster that occurs in a relatively short space of time. The descriptions in the narrative usually have an ethical subtext: the collapse is a divine and deserved punishment. It typically represents a divide between the old and a new age.

Such myths are described in detail in, for instance, ancient Egyptian literature and Near Eastern texts.[63] They usually have a moralizing core: unless an individual abides by a certain ethical code and behaves in accordance with the order of things mediated by the gods, just retribution will follow. We can, of course, only speculate about the historical and political contexts in which these myths arose, but it would be difficult not to imagine that one of the reasons must have been the authors' desire to seek meaning in the development of their society and find hope for renewal after a crisis, with its attendant decline in living standards, quality of governance, and technology, crafts, art, and trade. Like the examples here, collapse will be presented throughout this book as a transformation, a fundamental change, an intrinsic part of the development of society, and a means of regeneration and restoration once the system becomes largely defunct and unsatisfactory to the parties entering into the social contract.

One of the oldest descriptions of collapse and doom is found in the third millennium BC Sumerian *Epic of Gilgamesh*. Longer versions have been recorded in an old Babylonian composition, where the god Enki comes to Atrahases and tells him that the gods intend to flood the world to punish humans for their sins, and orders him to build an ark to save his family and other living creatures.[64]

The Bible contains a similar description. Here, for forty days the flood waters kept rising to destroy every living thing (Genesis 7:17–19, 24), after which new life began. This flood came as a punishment for the inappropriate behavior of people on earth and for their arrogance. The biblical account is almost identical to the Mesopotamian version.

Another famous text of collapse and doom is Plato's rendition of the tale of the mythical Atlantis, as preserved in the *Timaeus* and *Critias* dialogues. Plato (427–347 BC) describes the mythical continent of Atlantis as a model, ideal state in which, at first, people lived in harmony with the will of the gods. Later, however, they turned away from this order and began to desire more wealth and power, which ultimately led to their doom.

Ancient Egyptian literature also contains a myth about the destruction of humanity for plotting against the Egyptian gods, though the versions currently known have been dated much later than the Old Kingdom. The obdurate god Re orders Sekhmet, the goddess of war and destruction, to destroy humanity. But he relents in time and the human race is saved.

> It happened [in the time of the majesty of] Re, the self-created, after he had become king of men and gods together: Mankind plotted against him, while his majesty has grown old, his bones being silver, his flesh gold, and his hair true lapis-lazuli. . . .
> They (i.e., the gods) said to his majesty: Let your Eye go and smite them for you, those schemers of evil. No Eye is more able to smite them for you. May it go down as Hathor.
>   The goddess returned after slaying mankind in the desert, and the majesty of this god said: Welcome in peace, Hathor. Eye who did what I came for! Said the goddess: As you live for me, I have overpowered mankind, and it was balm to my heart. Said the majesty of Re: I shall power over them as king by diminishing them.[65]

These are the myths from ancient times as preserved through contemporary texts. But how did they come about and what did they mean to the people who actually listened to them? Did such disasters always mark an end, or can we consider them to be an inherent part of the historical process? And what options do archaeologists, historians, or environmental scientists have to study such disasters in the context of ancient Egypt, with the benefit of its written texts, religion, and complex social and state organization?

Ancient Egyptian history is said to have lasted for three thousand years. During that period, several empires emerged, peaked, and expired: the Old, Middle, and New Kingdoms, separated by intermediate periods (interregnums, which modern research shows were rife with local conflicts). The end of this development occurred in what is called the Late Period, which followed the New Kingdom. The final phase of Egyptian pharaonic rule was marked by two Persian conquests, in 525 and 343 BC, and Egypt's independence ended when the country was conquered for the third time by Alexander of Macedon in 332 BC. It was under Ptolemaic rule from 323 until 30 BC (Ptolemy was one of Alexander's successors who seized Egypt after his death), when it came under Roman domination. And yet, the language and religion lived on—albeit with many changes and modifications—practically until the fourth/fifth century AD.

While the individual kingdoms are characterized by economic, political, and intellectual expansion and the remarkable achievements of the human mind, the intermediate periods are less distinguished and bear clear signs of decline in the complexity of ancient Egyptian society. One interpretation might be that these were times of collapse, but they can also—and indeed preferably—be seen as a considerable simplification of the complexity of the system.

Nevertheless, the result is the same: a period of decline in the standard of living, of arts, crafts, and literature, and also a diminished ability by the state to carry out key tasks, which, in Egypt, involved defending the country's borders, building temples, collecting taxes, exercising the sovereign power of the king, and operating the redistributive system that was core to the economy and which provided the king and the ruling elite with legitimacy and superior status.[66] The central state apparatus fades out everywhere, the country disintegrates into smaller territorial units, and poverty spreads. All this is reflected on a general level, with only few exceptions, in the poor quality of grave goods found in cemeteries; there is evident leveling of the vertical structure of society.

A number of theories have been advanced to explain this decline, and in the next chapters, the following theses will be weighed:

- The Old Kingdom collapsed suddenly because of an internal coup or sudden 'revolution';
- The Old Kingdom collapsed due to a long-term, internal social, symbolic, and economic crisis of the state;
- The Old Kingdom collapsed quickly because of an invasion;
- The Old Kingdom collapsed due to the long-term effects of external factors, such as deteriorating climatic conditions and low Nile flooding;
- The Old Kingdom did not collapse at all; it is an illusion.[67]

We must also bear in mind that there may not be any single cause for a society's collapse, and that it is more likely to be a combination of various phenomena and long- and short-term trends working together. The next chapters will show how heterogenous and complicated was the process of non-linear evolution of ancient Egyptian society and how a number of phenomena played a role at different stages of development.

2 The River Nile and Egyptian History

CLIMATE AND CLIMATE CHANGE have had an omnipresent role in human development. Water and moisture can turn a desert into paradise; their absence can do the opposite. There is no life without water, and sooner or later people and societies start moving away from places where it is scarce. Ancient Egypt was no exception. Cultures and civilizations emerged in the Nile Valley because of the long-term drought of the Western and Eastern Deserts, and the Old Kingdom came to an end partly because of long-term aridification.[1]

The collapse of the Old Kingdom and other important entities in the Near East and elsewhere began at the same time: about 2200 BC.[2] The following pages will look at the climate change that took place in Egypt during the third millennium BC, focusing in particular on the main features of the period preceding that date.

Two extreme opinions seem to dominate the current debate around environmental change around 2200 BC.[3] The first is that there is no indication of climate change at that time. The second makes use of significant proxy data and defends the conclusion that many societies collapsed around this time due to a major deterioration in the climate.[4]

Nile Floods and the Palermo Stone

In Egypt, the main source of information on climate change is evidence about the rise and fall of the Nile. This phenomenon was, and in fact still is, the alpha and the omega of life in the valley. Nile flood levels were meticulously recorded until the completion of the Aswan High Dam in the 1960s, as the yearly measurement was of paramount importance in the Egyptian cyclical calendar.[5]

The earliest such data come from the early third millennium BC and are preserved on the Palermo Stone, and to a lesser extent on what is commonly called the South Saqqara stone.[6] The Palermo Stone was once part of a much larger monument that recorded the main events in each year of Egypt's existence as a unified country, from the advent of the first king of the First Dynasty to some time in the first half of the Fifth Dynasty, some six centuries later. It also listed the Predynastic rulers of (at least) Lower Egypt. The overall composition survives in seven fragments (not all of which necessarily come from the same original monument), but a substantial portion of the stone is lost.[7]

On its front side the Palermo Stone preserves a significant portion of the Royal Annals of the Old Kingdom. The space is divided into six horizontal registers inscribed with hieroglyphic texts running from right to left. The top register contains a list of Predynastic rulers of Lower Egypt. The following registers contain the names of the kings of unified Egypt, of the First to Fourth Dynasties. The second register starts with significant events in the last years of the rule of a First Dynasty king, probably Hor-Aha or Narmer, but the name is damaged. The details of Fifth Dynasty kings are on the back. Entries on the surviving fragments end with the reign of King Neferirkare, the third king of the Fifth Dynasty. In addition to the names of kings and the heights of yearly floods, the text includes the names of other members of the royal family, including the mothers of kings, who played a significant role in ancient Egyptian history, especially in matters of succession. Unfortunately, due to the way in which it is broken, it is not certain whether the record ended with King Neferirkare or continued for one or more later rulers.

The registers also record major events that occurred during each king's reign: the celebration of religious feasts, tax collection, the erection of statues in honor of different deities, building projects (often

Fig. 2.1. The Palermo Stone. (Photo courtesy Museo Archeologico Regionale di Palermo A. Salinas; photo M. Osman)

relating to the construction of royal palaces as major seats of the 'government'), military campaigns and the resulting booty, and details of the gifts (including land) that the king gave to individual temples, and, most important, the height of the Nile floods.

This was a phenomenon of extraordinary importance. The Nile flood season, *akhet* in the Egyptian calendar, marked a period of decreased agricultural activity—as the land was under water—when it became possible to transport heavy cargo by water across longer distances and into locations high above the normal level of the river. This was important especially in the transportation of large stone blocks from quarries as far south as Aswan—the origin of red granite, the most expensive building material in the Old Kingdom in terms of acquisition costs—to construction sites throughout Egypt, including the pyramid complexes of the kings.

Most revealing in this respect are the unique papyri discovered by the French archaeologist Pierre Tallet in Wadi al-Jarff on the coast of the Red Sea. They describe the transport of Tura limestone blocks (Tura was a major quarry for limestone for the Giza pyramids across the Nile) and date to the year 26 or 27 of King Khufu, which is the highest attested date for the reign of this ruler. This transport took place between July and November when the waters of the Nile were at their highest and the overland hauling of heavy cargo could be minimized.[8] One text preserved on the papyrus roll (papyrus B, Section B I) describes the daily routine of moving the stones by boat across the river during the inundation season:

> [Day 25]: [Inspector Merer spends the day with his phyle [h]au[ling]? st[ones in Tura South]; spends the night at Tura South [Day 26]: Inspector Merer casts o. with his phyle from Tura [South], loaded with stone, for Akhet-Khufu; spends the night at She-Khufu. Day 27: sets sail from She-Khufu, sails towards Akhet-Khufu, loaded with stone, spends the night at Akhet-Khufu. Day 28: casts o. from Akhet-Khufu in the morning; sails upriver <towards> Tura South. Day 29: Inspector Merer spends the day with his phyle hauling stones in Tura South; spends the night at Tura South. Day 30: Inspector Merer spends the day with his phyle hauling stones in Tura South; spends the night at Tura South.[9]

The height of the Nile flood was also a factor in the precise calculation of taxes from different types of fields across the country. Accurate measurement of the height of the flood was thus an inevitable part of the advance calculation of the tax yield from agriculture. An appropriate (neither too high nor too low) annual Nile flood was essential for the year's crops and thus for the output of the agriculture-based economy of the ancient Egyptians. Both too-low and too-high floods led to poor harvests and had a direct bearing on the state's economy.

Records of seventy-two floods—that is, seventy-two years of the Nile's history—are preserved on the Palermo Stone for the period from the First Dynasty until the middle of the Fifth Dynasty, specifically for the period from Djer to Neferirkare. This represents roughly 550 years, meaning that we have less than 13 percent of the expected number of records for the entire period. These are very limited data from which to conduct a detailed analysis of trends, but they do provide enough information to make basic observations.

Of the floods for which records survive, the largest number is concentrated during the First Dynasty: thirty-four entries altogether. The Second Dynasty has thirteen entries, and the Third Dynasty has fourteen. In contrast, only six have been preserved for the Fourth Dynasty and only five for the Fifth (from the reigns of Userkaf, Sahure, and Neferirkare). If the Palermo Stone did indeed contain data for every regnal year of every ruler, there would originally have been several hundred records. Within individual dynasties, the data are once again concentrated in the reigns of just a few kings: flood heights are documented for twelve different years during Djer's rule, thirteen during what has been estimated as Anedjib's rule, and the same for Ninetjer. As for the Old Kingdom, five entries have been preserved from what is estimated to be Djoser's reign, four from Sneferu's, and two from Khufu's.

The spread of the heights of individual floods is significant. The lowest are documented during the rule of King Ninetjer, only 0.52 meters (or exactly one cubit), and Anedjib, 1.04 meters. This latter is the third-lowest Nile flood for which we have records and is 0.5 meters higher than the documented lowest. The highest flood levels occurred during the reign of Anedjib, 4.22 and 3.55 meters, and Djer, 3.15 and 3.20 meters. There is no doubt that both the lowest and the highest floods had a devastating impact on the state's economy in those years.

It is interesting that records available from the time of King Anedjib testify to both extremely high and extremely low floods: the difference is more than three meters. The average inundation, judging from the entries preserved on the Palermo Stone, was approximately 2.04 meters. These data offer a clear view of the importance of floods to the ancient Egyptians and of the fact that the flooding was not just a monotonous annual event, but one that was anxiously awaited by everyone in Egypt.

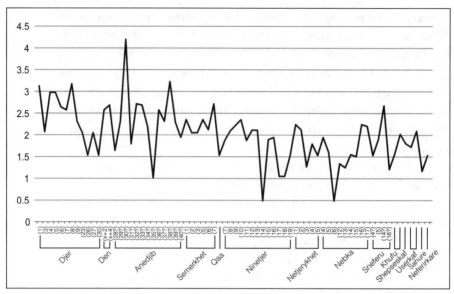

Fig. 2.2. Chart showing heights of the Nile floods as recorded on Palermo Stone. (compilation M. Bárta)

Although the Palermo Stone has been known since the mid-nineteenth century, it was not until the 1970s that the American Egyptologist Barbara Bell identified its great potential for the systematic evaluation of individual entries relating to the Nile floods.[10] Her study was followed and developed by Fekri Hassan in the 1980s.[11]

Interpreting details of the height of Nile floods has been difficult mainly because we do not know how or where the measurements recorded on the Palermo Stone were taken. But it is evident that this feature was measured continuously for several centuries and the acquired data systematically preserved.

One possibility, mentioned by Prince Omar Toussoun (1872–1944), a prominent member of the Egyptian royal family renowned for his scientific papers on the Nile and the Coptic monasteries in Wadi Natrun, is that these measurements were taken with a portable Nilometer, which during the periods between floods was kept in the temple of Apis (Toussoun refers to him as "Serapis") at Memphis. There is a report dating from the Greco-Roman period that describes a portable Nilometer, but it is possible that such a tool existed two thousand years earlier.[12]